london 360°

views inspired by british airways london eye

london 360°

views inspired by british airways london eye

Photographs by Jason Hawkes

additional photographs by Matt Livey

HarperCollins*Illustrated*

CONTENTS

 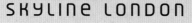

First published in 2000 by HarperCollins*Illustrated*
an imprint of HarperCollins*Publishers*
77-85 Fulham Palace Road
London W6 8JB

The HarperCollins website address is:
www.fireandwater.com

This book has been produced in conjunction with
British Airways London Eye

Text © HarperCollins*Publishers* 2000
Photographs © Jason Hawkes 2000

except page 6 © Nick Wood/Marks Barfield Architects
Eye icons © HarperCollins*Publishers* 2000
pages 26–8, 29(b), 34–5, 37–8, 43, 48–9, 51, 53–4, 57,
59(r), 60–61, 66(r), 70(r), 79–80, 86(r), 88, 92(l), 94(b),
97(l), 98, 100–101, 102(b&r), 103(b), 106–7, 109–111,
112–15, 117–19, 120–5, 127 © Matt Livey 2000

A CIP catalogue record for this book
is available from the British Library

ISBN: 0 00 220208 5

Design and artworks: Tanya Devonshire-Jones

04 02 00 01 03
2 4 6 8 9 7 5 3 1

Colour reproduction by Colourscan, Singapore
Printed and bound in the UK
by Montgomery Litho Group

AMAZING PERSPECTIVES

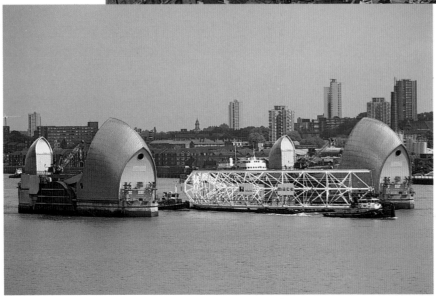

PREPARING FOR TAKE-OFF

British Airways London Eye lay flat out into the River Thames before being raised to its vertical position. Here we see the final rim section being added – an exciting moment in summer 1999.

BRINGING IT ALL TOGETHER

The components were shipped up the River Thames to be assembled on the South Bank. Here sections of the rim negotiate the silver Thames Barrier in Docklands.

A BREATHTAKING SCALE

The capsules, with their innovative design by David Marks & Julia Barfield Architects, can hold up to 25 people. These images give some idea of the sheer scale of the strucutre.

THE REAL THING

British Airways London Eye was raised to its dominant position on the South Bank in October 1999. It is the capital's 4th tallest structure and dwarfs the buildings that surround it.

INTRODUCTION

FOREWORD
BY JASON HAWKES

Battersea Heliport. London. 6.45pm. I'll finish loading the cameras and check the exposure meter. Double check my safety harness and then confirm the door is locked open – it will remain open for the duration of the two-hour flight over London. Headsets on and check the pilot can hear me OK. Position myself at the edge of the door with one foot on the skid of the helicopter. The twin jet engines roar as they burst into life and we hover taxi to the pontoon over the river. A final check with Battersea Control Tower and we start our backwards ascent (if we have a engine failure now we should be able to land back on the pontoon without too much trouble) to around 250 ft before swinging out over the Thames. Climbing quickly to 750 ft for safety we cruise down to the House of Commons, our first location to begin the shoot.

Flying over London is indeed a rare pleasure. You get an overall view of the whole capital, whilst at the same time being able to gain insights into places usually unseen. Hovering here 500 ft above Big Ben, concentrating upon a suitable composition, you can't help but notice the huge terrace scattered with tables which overlooks the Thames, where our MPs gather to enjoy an evening drink. Where else but from a helicopter could you see the extraordinary 'village' of buildings on top of Harrods, look down upon 10 Downing Street and see the beautiful gardens of Buckingham Palace, all within the space of ten minutes.

From the Houses of Parliament we cross the river to the site of the magnificent British Airways London Eye. We settle down to a fairly blustery hover, and for the next half an hour of photography I experience the wonderful view that people will have from the capsules of London's latest landmark.

During the days leading up to the shoot I will have gone through our flight plan with air traffic control to obtain a 'Whiskey number', which should, once activated, give us access to our locations over the capital. A twin-engined helicopter is needed to fly here under the Civil Aviation Authority regulations and at £850 per hour it is certainly not cheap. However, all the technicalities are now behind us and I must concentrate on obtaining the images I need while

at the same time taking in the breathtaking experience and incredible freedom of flying over the capital.

Rush hour does not exist up here. Traffic jams and congested tube lines are not our concern. We can cruise at over 120 mph as the whole city unveils itself below us. One moment we're flying at 1000 ft over Oxford Circus, the next we're circling Canary Wharf, negotiating the capital faster than even the most nimble of motorcycle couriers.

We circle the Isle of Dogs as I shout directions through my headset to Jessy the pilot, battling with the thunderous noise of the engine and the rotating blades above us. He settles us into a hover around 150 ft above the pinnacle of Canada Tower in Canary Wharf. Below us, the windows of the shimmering Tower's 45 floors reflect the evening sunlight and the building, like an enormous sundial, casts its vast shadow across North Greenwich, the Millennium Dome and beyond.

We will fly from location to location, the pilot in constant contact with either Heathrow Special or City Airport Control, as we slowly pick off the subjects for the book. Occasionally we will be asked to move away, perhaps to let a commercial jet come in to land or take off from City Airport. Today it's a rather more urgent matter – we see the sleek orange air ambulance from Whitechapel Hospital in the East End whisk underneath us to yet another emergency.

The sun slowly sinks lower in the sky and bathes the city in its orange glow. One or two more locations and it will be time to head back west along the Thames, out past the giant reservoirs at Barnes, and over the static traffic jams on the Hammersmith Flyover. We'll slow down one last time to close the large sliding door on the helicopter before climbing back up to 1500 ft and speeding along at 140 mph for the short trip back through the countryside to Booker airfield. The end of another day.

The photographs in this book represent some of the most exciting views you can experience from British Airways London Eye, starting with four fantastic panoramas of the whole of London and beyond.

LOOKING NORTH

1	BT Tower	6	Bedford Square	10	Adelphi Hotel
2	Embankment Place	7	Embankment Gardens	11	Russell Square
3	Charing Cross	8	Senate House	12	Covent Garden Market
4	Centrepoint		(University of London)	13	Royal Opera House
5	Hampstead Heath	9	British Museum	14	New British Library

LOOKING EAST

LOOKING SOUTH

1	Lambeth Palace	7	Millbank Tower	11	The Atrium
2	MI6 Headquarters	8	New Covent Garden	12	House of Lords
3	Alembic House		Market	13	The Terrace
4	Lambeth Bridge	9	Tate Britain	14	Battersea Power
5	Vauxhall Bridge	10	Victoria Tower		Station
6	River Thames		Gardens	15	Battersea Park

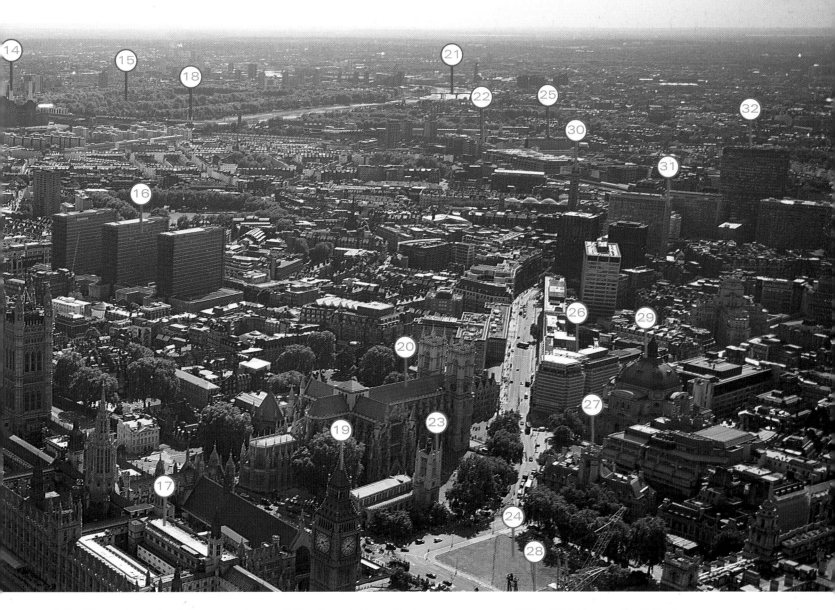

16	Department of Transport	22	Royal Hospital, Chelsea	27	Middlesex Guildhall
17	House of Commons	23	St Margaret's Church	28	Churchill Statue
18	Chelsea Bridge	24	Parliament Square	29	Central Methodist Hall
19	Big Ben	25	Victoria Station	30	Westminster Cathedral
20	Westminster Abbey	26	New Scotland Yard	31	Westminster City Hall
21	Albert Bridge			32	Portland House

LOOKING WEST

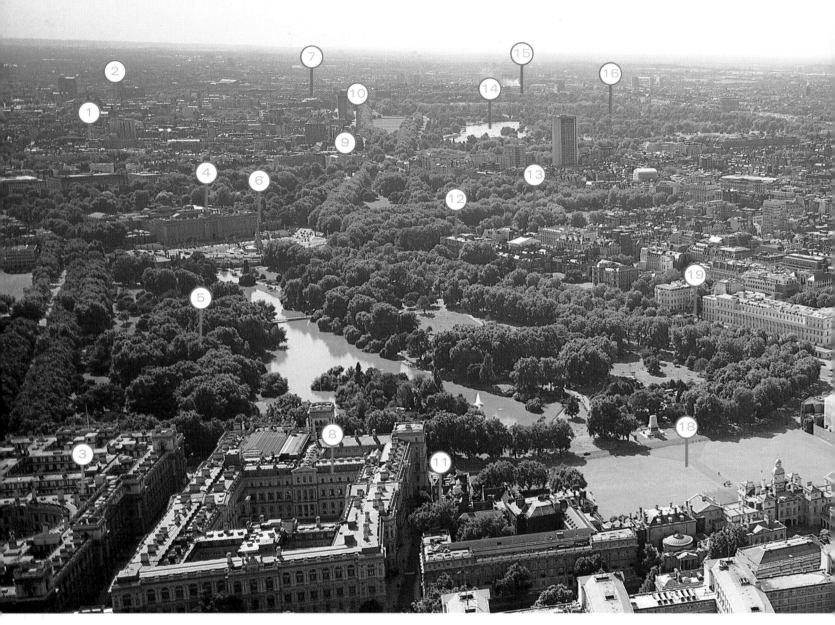

1	Victoria & Albert	5	St James's Park	11	Downing Street
	Museum	6	Victoria Memorial	12	Clarence House
2	Natural History	7	Royal Albert Hall	13	Green Park
	Museum	8	Foreign Office	14	The Serpentine
3	HM Treasury	9	Hyde Park Corner	15	Kensington Palace
4	Buckingham Palace	10	Harrods	16	Hyde Park

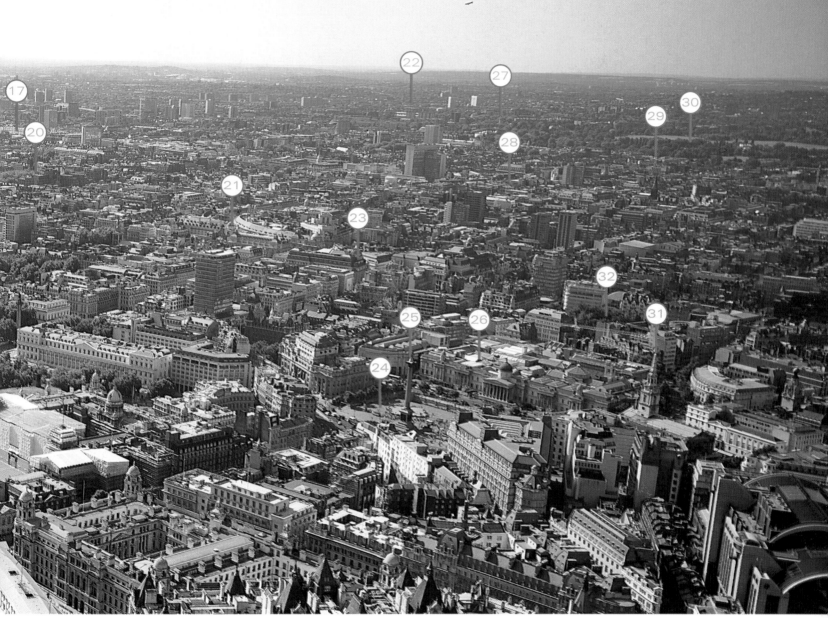

THE RIVER
THAMES

THE RIVER THAMES LOOKING EAST

The importance of the Thames to London can clearly be seen, as it meanders downstream past Tower Bridge and Docklands. Two domes and two towers stand out, reflecting the ancient and the modern: the Tower of London and Canada Tower at Canary Wharf; the famous dome of St Paul's Cathedral and, further downriver, Richard Rogers' Millennium Dome.

TOWER BRIDGE

A view over HMS Belfast to Tower Bridge and the dominant presence of London's tallest building, Canada Tower on the Isle of Dogs. To the left of Tower Bridge is the Tower of London, once a fortress, palace and prison and now one of the capital's greatest tourist attractions.

THE RIVER LOOKING WEST

Here in the foreground we see Battersea Park on the south bank of the river, and its beautiful Peace Pagoda. On the opposite bank is Chelsea Royal Hospital where every May hoards of green-fingered gardening devotees descend upon the world-renowned Chelsea Flower Show.

HMS BELFAST

Looking from the air like a toy battleship, HMS Belfast was built in 1939, and at 11,000 tons is the largest cruiser ever built for the Royal Navy. She is now permanently moored at Symon's Wharf where she is open to the public as part of the Imperial War Museum.

COVENT GARDEN AND THE RIVER

A view across the elegant rooftops of Covent Garden towards the river and south across the boroughs of Lambeth and Southwark. Lambeth became renowned for its pottery (Royal Doulton started life here, as Doulton and Watts) and Southwark was famous as the cradle of Elizabethan theatre.

BATTERSEA POWER STATION

Here we look down into the gutted shell of Sir Giles Gilbert Scott's vast power station. It featured on the cover of Pink Floyd's famous 'Animals' album, where an inflatable pig was photographed attached to one of the chimneys. Scott also designed one of the most familiar sights in London and Britain – the K6, otherwise known as the red telephone box.

THE THAMES BARRIER

The futuristic machine housings of the Thames Barrier gleam in the sunshine. Here we see just the tip – most of this gargantuan flood barrier is underwater.

THE MILLENNIUM DOME

Standing 50 metres tall and covering 80,000 square metres, the Dome is large enough to hold the Eiffel Tower lying on its side. In the right-hand photograph the pet hate of many motorists, the Blackwall tunnel, lies deep underneath the upper bend of the River.

BRIDGES

PARLIAMENT BY NIGHT

Sunset provides a spectacular backdrop to Westminster Bridge and the Palace of Westminster, better known as the Houses of Parliament. The view from the bridge's predecessor was celebrated in Wordsworth's 1802 poem, *Lines Written upon Westminster Bridge*; 'Earth has not anything to show more fair: Dull would he be of soul who could pass by a sight so touching in its majesty...'.

SOUTH OVER WESTMINSTER BRIDGE

Across the broad sweep of the bridge, remarkable for its time, is the colonnaded crescent of County Hall, and beyond that the Shell Centre, officially known as the Downstream Building. When the first Westminster Bridge was built from 1738-50, the nearest river crossings were at Putney Bridge and London Bridge.

TOWER BRIDGE

Tower Bridge is only just over 100 years old and yet, with the possible exception of Big Ben, it is London's most famous landmark. These views highlight the strength and gothic splendour of Sir Horace Jones' bridge, which was a triumph of engineering with its overhead footbridges and the elevating arms of the roadway. Until they were electrified in 1976, the bascules (from the French for see-saw) were raised by steam-powered hydraulics which failed only once – at the opening ceremony!

GIRL WITH A DOLPHIN

David Wynne's *Girl with a Dolphin* (1973).
From this perspective, the dolphin's graceful
back matches the curve of the girders while
the swimmer seems to float weightlessly in
the sky above Tower Bridge.

EMBANKMENT PLACE AND HUNGERFORD BRIDGE

Trains running from south London across the Hungerford Bridge terminate at Charing Cross. Passengers leaving Charing Cross can enjoy a great view of British Airways London Eye, Westminster and the Houses of Parliament.

BRIDGES TO THE EAST

In the foreground is London's newest art gallery, Tate Modern, a haven for modern art lovers, and formerly the Bankside Power Station. The three bridges spanning the Thames here are, from west to east, Southwark Bridge, Cannon Street railway bridge and London Bridge.

ALBERT BRIDGE

Albert Bridge, which was first opened in 1873, joins Battersea on the south bank to the wealthy borough of Kensington and Chelsea to the north. The luminous white bridge has a serene quality to it and is one of the capital's most beautiful bridges.

THE RIVER
LOOKING WEST

Julius Caesar is reputed to have crossed the Thames here in the year 55 BC – without the benefit of the two bridges which now link Battersea Park to Chelsea. At the end of the last century, the park was crowded with people who went there to practice the new craze of bicycling (or simply to watch). Today the park remains a peaceful sanctuary from the bustle of London life which crowds its boundaries.

RIVER BANKS

THE VICTORIA EMBANKMENT

Here we look north across the river towards the Victoria Embankment, which was reclaimed from the Thames at the end of the 19th century. Hungerford Bridge takes the railway into Charing Cross Station beneath the jukebox-like frontage of Embankment Place. Villiers Street runs to the right of the station, and marks the site of Hungerford Market, where Charles Dickens was employed filling jars with boot polish from the age of 11.

CLEOPATRA'S NEEDLE

Cleopatra's Needle is London's oldest monument, being one of a pair erected in Egypt c.1475 BC – the other one is in New York. The granite obelisk was presented to Britain in 1819 to celebrate the British victory over the French in Egypt, and has a Victorian time capsule buried beneath it containing various objects of the day. The Needle is guarded by two Victorian sphinxes.

BANKSIDE AND THE GLOBE THEATRE

The reconstruction of Shakespeare's Globe Theatre, close to the site of the original, has rejuvenated the Bankside area, as have the conversion of the Bankside power station into the capital's newest art gallery, Tate Modern, and the building of the Millennium Bridge – London's first bridge across the Thames since Tower Bridge was opened.

COUNTY HALL

This is the turret of County Hall, which was originally designed to house the London County Council and was opened in 1922. It achieved its greatest moment of fame as the headquarters of the Greater London Council during the 1980s.

THE LONDON AQUARIUM

The crescent of County Hall towers above the Aquarium, which is laid out across three floors of County Hall's basement (and includes a `touch pool' where children can handle hermit crabs, starfish and rays).

THE SOUTH BANK LION

This statue started life as a red lion which stood over the entrance arch to the Lion Brewery near Hungerford Bridge. When the French novelist Emile Zola saw it in 1893 he wrote that: 'It amused me greatly, this British Lion waiting to wish me good morning.'

THE HOUSES OF PARLIAMENT

The Gothic Houses of Parliament, built by Sir Charles Barry, and the clock tower, 'Big Ben', are two of London's true icons – instantly recognisable across the globe. The building, which covers 8 acres, was completed in 1860. The bell inside the clock tower weighs 13.5 tonnes.

THE RAF MEMORIAL

A gold eagle spreads its wings to fly skywards from its stone plinth, with the inscription: 'I bare (sic) you on eagle's wings and brought you unto myself'. In memory of 'the men and women of the air forces of every part of the British Commonwealth and Empire' who gave their lives in the two world wars.

VICTORIA EMBANKMENT

This fierce-looking sea monster is coiled round the base of a streetlamp, one of many such elaborate iron lamp standards which line the riverside along the Victoria Embankment.

SKYLINE
LONDON

A CHANGING SKYLINE

From the colourful swirl of the IMAX cinema in the foreground to the distant gleam of the Thames Barrier, glass and steel dominate London's modern architecture, while more traditional landmarks such as Tower Bridge and St Paul's retain their splendour, instantly recognisable amongst surroundings which have radically changed with the centuries.

CLASSIC SKYLINE

ST PAUL'S CATHEDRAL

It is the dome of St Paul's Cathedral which characterises the London skyline, but from the air the cruciform shape of the cathedral becomes apparent. Christopher Wren caused enormous controversy in his day with his plans for the dome, which was thought to be quite unsuitable for an English cathedral.

BIG BEN

The Clock Tower is known throughout the world as Big Ben, although the name actually refers to the huge 13.5-ton bell which chimes the hour. The bell is thought to be named after either Sir Benjamin Hall, Chief Commissioner of Works at the time it was made, or Benjamin Caunt, a popular heavyweight boxer, who weighed 18 stone.

THE NATWEST TOWER (TOWER 42)

From above the tower, and looking directly down upon the cooling fans which crown the building you will see that the outline shape is that of the NatWest logo. This view looks east to the Tower of London and, in the far distance, Canary Wharf and Docklands.

CANARY WHARF

Cesar Pelli's spectacular stainless steel and glass skyscraper towers 800 ft above the Isle of Dogs and can be seen from as far afield as Kent and Essex. Canary Wharf is actually the name of the strip of land where tomatoes and bananas used to be landed from the Canary Islands. The tower itself, Europe's second tallest building after Frankfurt's Messerturm, is officially known as One Canada Square.

WEST END SKYLINE

CENTREPOINT

Centrepoint dominates the intersection of Oxford Street and Charing Cross Road. One of the West End's tallest landmarks, this office complex looks down upon the armies of Londoners and tourists as they make their way through some of the capital's busiest shopping streets.

THE BT TOWER

The distinctive shape of the BT Tower – still known to many as the Post Office Tower – rises above the surrounding buildings of Fitzrovia and the greenery of Regent's Park. The tower is actually a huge 620-ft pylon, supporting radio, television and telecoms aerials and a weather radar.

THE POWER
AND THE GLORY

WESTMINSTER ABBEY

An awesome perspective of the North Front of the Abbey, built for Henry III and inspired by the cathedrals of Amiens and Rheims. The Abbey is an integral part of the history of England — William the Conqueror was crowned here, as was every monarch since, apart from Edwards V and VIII, neither of whom was crowned.

THE CHURCH

LAMBETH PALACE

Built in 1490, Lambeth Palace stands on the south bank of the River Thames between Westminster Bridge and Lambeth Bridge and is home to the Archbishop of Canterbury. The Great Hall houses the world-renowned Lambeth Palace Library.

WESTMINSTER ABBEY

The towers of the magnificent West Front of Westminster Abbey reach skywards. In the nave beyond this grand entrance lies the Tomb of the Unknown Soldier, commemorating the one million British soldiers who died in the First World War.

CHRIST CHURCH, SPITALFIELDS

The largest of Hawksmoor's churches stands on Commercial Road opposite Spitalfields market. The areas of Brick Lane, Shoreditch and Hoxton, which surround the church, have become among the most fashionable in London, with new bars and cafés opening as the fashion-conscious make their homes in the newly converted warehouses.

LONDON CENTRAL MOSQUE

The colonnade, dome and minaret of London Central Mosque stand out from the green of Regent's Park. The mosque is an eminently suitable addition to a park designed for the Prince Regent (later George IV), whose taste for the Orient is to be seen in his most extravagant artistic project, the Brighton Pavilion.

ST PAUL'S CATHEDRAL

St Paul's Cathedral, which became a symbol of hope and defiance for Londoners during the Blitz, is lit theatrically against a clear twilight sky. After Henry VIII's dissolution of the monasteries, much of the revenue from the Abbey of St Peter (Westminster Abbey) was transferred to St Paul's, which is the origin of the phrase 'robbing Peter to pay Paul'.

GOVERNMENT AND JUSTICE

THE HOUSES OF PARLIAMENT

A rare bird's-eye view into the courtyards of the Palace of Westminster, which has been the home of the Houses of Parliament since the reign of Edward VI. Much of the Gothic detail of Parliament (below) is by Augustus Pugin, whose life reads like the plot of a Gothic novel – shipwrecked in 1830, married in 1831, lost his wife in 1832, married again in 1833, lost his second wife in 1844, married again in 1849, lost his mind in 1851 and died in Bedlam mental hospital in 1852.

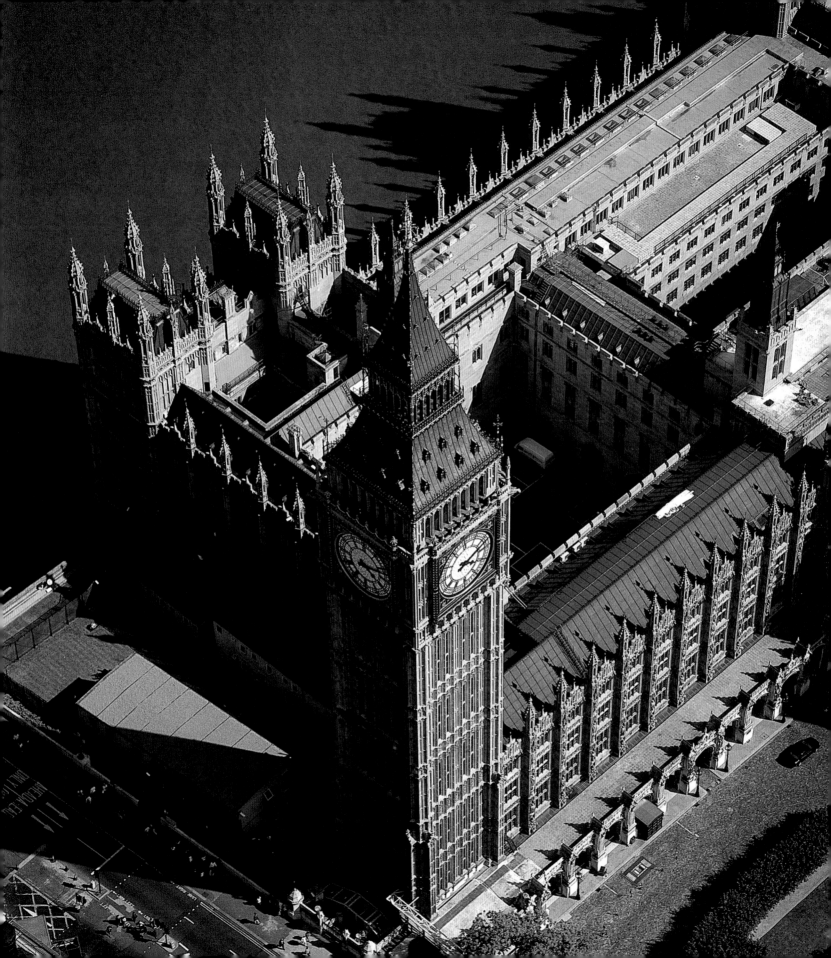

BUCKINGHAM PALACE

Somewhat surprisingly, the Palace has been the monarch's official home for less than 200 years. The present Queen is Colonel-in-Chief of the 7 Household Regiments which still form part of the regular British army, as well as performing ceremonies such as the Changing of the Guard.

THE ROYAL COURTS OF JUSTICE

A huge complex of more than fifty courtrooms including the Court of Appeal and the High Court. Carey Street runs along the north side of the complex and used to be the site of the bankruptcy court, hence the phrase 'going to Carey Street' for those of unsound finances.

Defence

THE TOWER OF LONDON

'Send him to the Tower!' The place of the Tower in the history, myth and legend of London is unsurpassed. As one American author noted, 'It is to poisoning, hanging, beheading, regicide, and torture what Yankee Stadium is to baseball.' Seen here from the air, the Tower retains its sense of aloof, unruffled power even amongst the traffic and office buildings of modern London – and the Tower still has a modern role to play in the safekeeping of the Crown Jewels.

HEN · VIII · REGE · FVNDATVM · CIVIVM · LARGITAS · PERFECIT

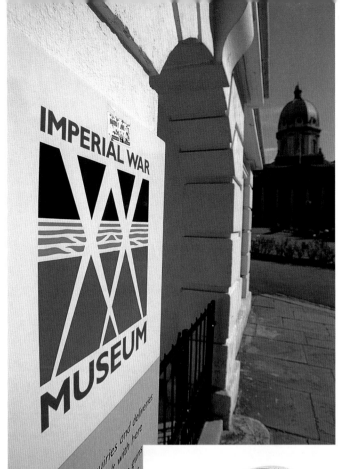

THE IMPERIAL WAR MUSEUM

The suitably imposing facade of the Imperial War Museum is flanked by 15-inch shells, ammunition for the impressive guns which once saw action on *HMS Resolution* and *HMS Ramillies*. The building was previously part of the Bethlehem Royal Hospital, better known as the mental hospital Bedlam, where Charlie Chaplin's mother was amongst the inmates.

MI6 HEADQUARTERS

For the headquarters of a secret intelligence service, the MI6 building is not exactly secretive, and even makes an appearance in a James Bond movie. Terry Farrell's postmodernist ziggurat (reportedly connected to Whitehall by a tunnel beneath the river) is often thought to be the headquarters of MI5, which is in fact housed at Thames House on Millbank.

MI6, OVAL AND KENNINGTON

From the air the depth of the MI6 building is surprising compared with the foreshortened view to be had on the ground. Across the road from MI6 is Big Bob, the world's largest tethered helium balloon, which could claim to be London's highest viewpoint prior to the raising of British Airways London Eye.

LONDON
AT WORK

THE CITY

Here we see the financial heartland of London, commonly known as the Square Mile. At its heart is the Lloyds Building, built by Richard Rogers. The building, designed in 1979, is a radical and starkly beautiful construction. Love it or hate it, you can't ignore it.

THE CITY

THE NATWEST TOWER (TOWER 42)

The NatWest Tower, now officially known as Tower 42, is a colossal symbol of financial power rising high above the City of London. When it was completed in 1980, it was Europe's tallest building, at 600 ft high. It stands on the site of Thomas Gresham's house, financial adviser to Elizabeth I and the man who first suggested the idea of a Royal Exchange.

BANK STATION

Bank is at the heart of the Square Mile – the world's top financial centre, dominating Europe in shares and foreign exchange, leading the world in futures and options, and remaining part of a global triumvirate of money markets along with New York and Tokyo.

THE LLOYDS BUILDING

Lloyds, one of the most traditional City institutions, commissioned Richard Rogers to design its avant-garde headquarters. The building is still attended by porters in waiters' livery – a reminder of the company's origins as a coffee house.

LIVERPOOL STREET

Thousands of slickly suited commuters will alight here daily and head for the maze of modern office developments around Broadgate, just behind the station, or continue their journey on the numerous other tube lines that pass through this bustling City thoroughfare.

ST KATHARINE DOCKS

Fifty years ago St Katharine Docks was a hive of activity as a centre for the Thames maritime traffic. Built in 1828 by Thomas Telford, the ships are now yachts and the warehouses gentrified flats and offices.

THE WEST END

CENTREPOINT AND THE WEST END

Here we look past the Centrepoint building to Tottenham Court Road. In the distance, London's third tallest building, the BT Tower, dominates the skyline. The BT Tower once housed a revolving restaurant in the sky, but this was sadly closed in 1971 following a bomb attack.

PICCADILLY CIRCUS

Piccadilly's remarkable Eros statue is not actually Eros at all – the statue is not the god of love but the Angel of Christian Charity, a memorial to the philanthropist Lord Shaftesbury.

OXFORD STREET AND MARBLE ARCH

The world's busiest and arguably most famous shopping street cuts a two-mile swathe through the West End (left). The old Roman road to Oxford attracts millions of visitors and provides employment for those who work in its shops and department stores. At the west end of Oxford Street stands Marble Arch, which used to form the entrance to Buckingham Palace until it was discovered that it was too narrow for the royal coaches to pass through!

LANGHAM PLACE

To many BBC radio listeners Langham Place is the centre of the world, dominated as it is by Broadcasting House, which looms over the distinctive circular portico of the Church of All Souls. Across the road is a hotel familiar to readers of Sherlock Holmes – the Langham Hilton, whose guests have included the composer Dvořák and exiled emperors Napoleon III and Haile Selassie.

DOCKLANDS AND THE EAST END

DOCKLANDS AND CANARY WHARF

The shimmering Canada Tower and the Canary Wharf development in Docklands were designed to be part of the regeneration of the Isle of Dogs, which was once one of the most run-down areas of London's East End. The Conservative government gave unrestricted building rights to the London Dockland Development Corporation in 1981 and since then the area has been transformed beyond all recognition and is now graced by some of the capital's most impressive and innovative modern architecture.

RIVERSIDE HOUSING

Shad Thames is an area on the south bank of the river where much new housing is being developed. Beautiful old warehouses with huge timber frames have been renovated to provide apartments with stunning river views. London's Design Museum and a handful of Conran restaurants add to the area's appeal.

THE MILLENNIUM DOME

Richard Rogers' grand statement to usher in the second millennium is by far the world's largest dome, 50 metres high and with a circumference of over half a mile. Detractors of the Dome, particularly those who decry a `temporary' structure, should bear in mind that the Eiffel Tower was only designed to last the duration of the 1889 Exposition in Paris.

SPITALFIELDS

Visit Spitalfields' vibrant market on a Sunday morning, perhaps after
an early morning walk to nearby Columbia Road flower market. Here
young fashion designers vie for space with organic fruit juice stalls.
The Spitalfields building is fast being swept up by the ever advancing
tidal wave of the City, as new office blocks hem in from all sides.

LONDON'S FAMOUS MARKETS

At the other end of the spectrum from Oxford Street are London's street markets, giving a feel of what London was like when it was still a collection of self-contained communities. Two of the most famous are Brick Lane (left), where the bricks were produced which helped to rebuild London after the Great Fire, and the flower market in nearby Columbia Road (below).

COLUMBIA ROAD E2

GETTING THERE

BY RIVER

Boats regularly ply their way between Westminster and Greenwich, calling at Charing Cross and Tower Pier en route. Some people use them to commute, but they are seen mainly as pleasure cruises for tourists. However, plans for a new river-bus system should help integrate all London's different modes of transport.

BY BUS

London's old red Routemaster was once to London what the yellow cab is to New York. But the Routemaster is no longer king, being replaced on many routes by modern buses in the liveries of the various private companies which share the network.

CLAPHAM JUNCTION

This mesh of railway lines, with tiny plastic people dotted around the platform and cardboard whitewashed signalling sheds alongside the tracks, looks just like a boy's model train set. First opened in 1863, the station is now one of London's busiest.

BY TUBE

London's tube network was the world's first underground railway system and is still the most extensive, covering an area of 630 square miles and operating over 254 miles of track. The concept has been copied in cities the world over, not least in Paris, whose Metro echoes the name of London's first underground line, the Metropolitan.

WATERLOO INTERNATIONAL STATION

The panels of Nicholas Grimshaw's glass roof look like the plates of a gigantic insect carapace as they follow the twists and curves of the track at Waterloo. The noses of four Eurostar trains emerge from the canopy, which shelters one of the longest railway platforms in the world.

CHARING CROSS STATION & EMBANKMENT PLACE

Embankment Place houses not only Charing Cross Station but also 9 floors of offices for over 3,000 people. More than 800 train services wind their way to Charing Cross daily, disgorging their passengers onto the busy streets of Covent Garden and the Strand.

STREETS,
SQUARES
AND SPACES

REGENT'S PARK

Originally part of the vast forest of Middlesex, Regent's Park is an oasis of green among the sprawl of London's buildings, with Bedford College nestling among the trees in the foreground.

SQUARES

LEICESTER SQUARE

Named after Robert Sidney, the 2nd Earl of Leicester, the Square became a place of entertainment during the 19th century, when Turkish baths and oyster houses appeared, as well as music halls such as the Empire and the Hippodrome, which today are a cinema and a disco.

TRAFALGAR SQUARE

Nelson's statue appears tiny atop his 145-ft granite column, although
the figure is in fact three times life size. This elevated view reveals the
clutter of rooftops behind the elegant Neoclassical facade of the
National Gallery, with the new Sainsbury Wing to the left. Trafalgar
Square has been the focus for political demonstrations since the
Chartists, and is the scene of London's annual New Year celebrations.

COVENT GARDEN MARKET HALL

Today, Covent Garden is a lively shopping area with performances from street entertainers and buskers – the area is so named because it was once the garden of a convent attached to the abbey of St Peter at Westminster. Later, a fruit and vegetable market was established and eventually a market hall was built which gives Covent Garden its unique character.

COVENT GARDEN PIAZZA

The twin glass roofs of Covent Garden's market hall are a relatively recent addition to the piazza which was originally laid out in the 1630s by Inigo Jones and was based on the main square of the town of Livorno in Italy.

STREETS

DOWNING STREET

Sir George Downing would probably have been surprised at the fame generated by his modest terrace of plain brick houses. Here we have a rare glimpse into the garden of Number 10, which also reveals that behind the famous front door the house is connected to a much larger, L-shaped building at the rear.

LONDON PLANETARIUM AND MADAME TUSSAUD'S

The green dome of the Planetarium is a strange addition to the architecture of Marylebone Road – lift the lid and you will see a display of the earth and its place in the solar system. Next door is the world-famous Madame Tussaud's gallery of wax models.

KING'S ROAD

The King's Road is literally what this was – Charles II had it built as a private route to avoid congestion on the public roads! It was eventually opened to the public and reached its height of fame in the swinging sixties as the centre of London fashion, along with Carnaby Street. On the south side of King's Road is Royal Avenue, where James Bond had his London address.

THE MALL

The original Mall was created in about 1660, and replaced Pall Mall as the alley for playing the game of the same name. At the start of the 20th century, as part of a memorial to Queen Victoria, The Mall was laid out as a wide, processional route leading from Admiralty Arch to Buckingham Palace. The original Mall can still be seen forming the adjoining horse ride.

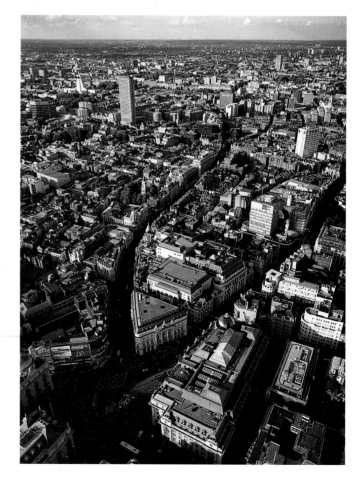

SHAFTESBURY AVENUE

Shaftesbury Avenue curves gently towards Bloomsbury from Piccadilly Circus, separating Soho from Chinatown. The Avenue, named after the 19th-century philanthropist Lord Shaftesbury, is at the heart of Theatreland, with six theatres and two cinemas along its length, including the Shaftesbury Theatre at its north-eastern end.

ROYAL PARKS

London is more than a dense, built-up city –
the many parks, royal and otherwise, provide
hundreds of acres of green, open space within
the capital. The centrepiece of Regent's Park is
Queen Mary's Rose Garden within the Inner
Circle; other attractions include the Y-shaped
boating lake, the Open Air Theatre and
London Zoo. As with most of London's royal
parks, Regent's Park (above and right) and
Hyde Park (left) are both laid out on land
that was seized from the church by Henry VIII
in order to provide himself with ever more
hunting grounds.

PARKS AND
OPEN SPACES

KENSINGTON GARDENS

A stroll through Hyde Park along the beautiful Serpentine lake to the edge of Kensington Gardens takes you past the recently refurbished Albert Memorial (left). Queen Victoria had the memorial built in 1870 to mark the death of her beloved husband, Prince Albert. Across Kensington Gore is the Royal Albert Hall (right). Built in 1871, it remains London's most inspiring concert venue.

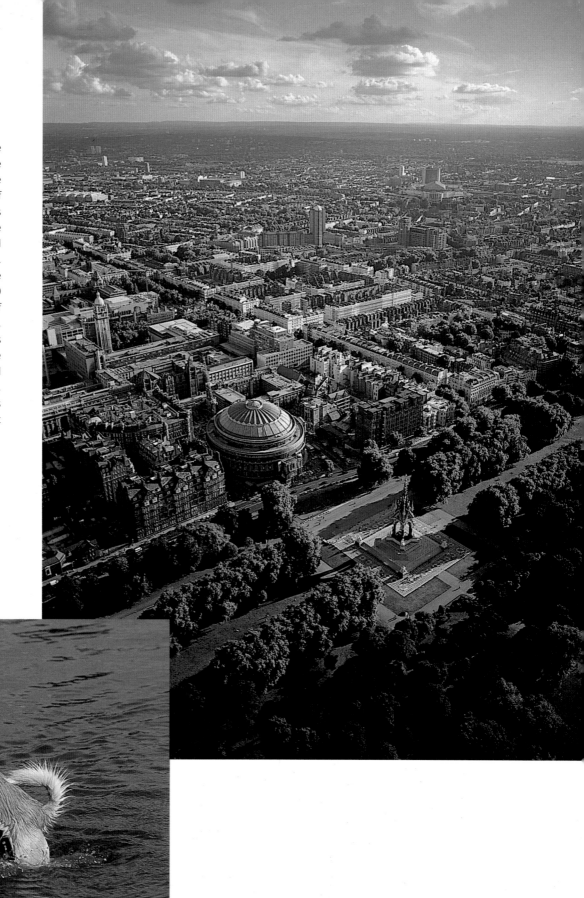

BATTERSEA PARK AND THE PEACE PAGODA

The Peace Pagoda sits in the sunshine among the trees of Battersea Park, overlooking the riverfront. A gift from Japanese Buddhists, the Pagoda was accepted by the Greater London Council in 1984 as part of their Peace Year, and was completed in May 1985. It is one of seventy such pagodas to be built around the world in the name of peace.

CLAPHAM COMMON

The 220 acres of Clapham Common have long been an area of rest and relaxation for south Londoners, and an arena for informal sports – including a hopping match held there in 1827! Harriet Westbrook attended a school on Clapham Common from which she eloped in 1811 to become the first wife of the poet Shelley.

LONDON
AT LEISURE

THE SOUTH BANK

In 1951 the South Bank Exhibition formed the centrepiece of the Festival of Britain and led to the eventual creation of the South Bank Centre, which includes, from right to left, the Royal Festival Hall, Queen Elizabeth Hall, Hayward Gallery, National Film Theatre and National Theatre. The 1951 exhibition included a ferris wheel and the Dome of Discovery, precursors of the millennium creations for the year 2000.

entertainment

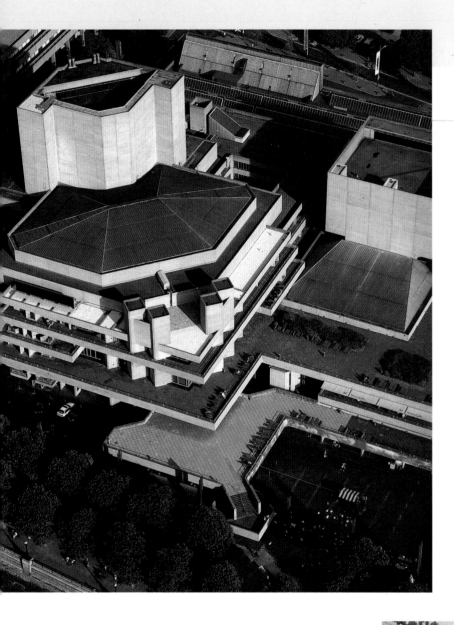

THE NATIONAL THEATRE

The idea of a national theatre was first suggested in 1848 but only finally came to fruition in 1976, after foundation stones had been laid on four separate occasions. Denys Lasdun's concrete edifice houses the three theatres which make up the NT: the large, open-stage Olivier; the more traditional proscenium stage of the Lyttelton, and the Cottesloe studio theatre.

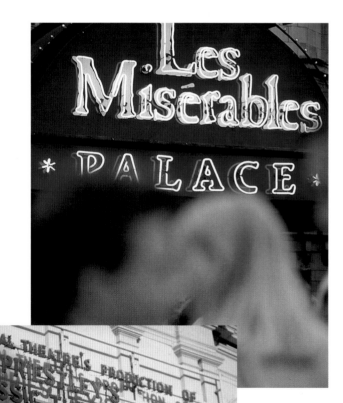

WEST END SHOWS

London's West End theatres are world famous for the Victorian splendour of the buildings and for the excellent shows performed there. In recent times, the West End has become synonymous with musicals but there are a host of straight plays, including *The Mousetrap*, with its world-record run which began in 1952.

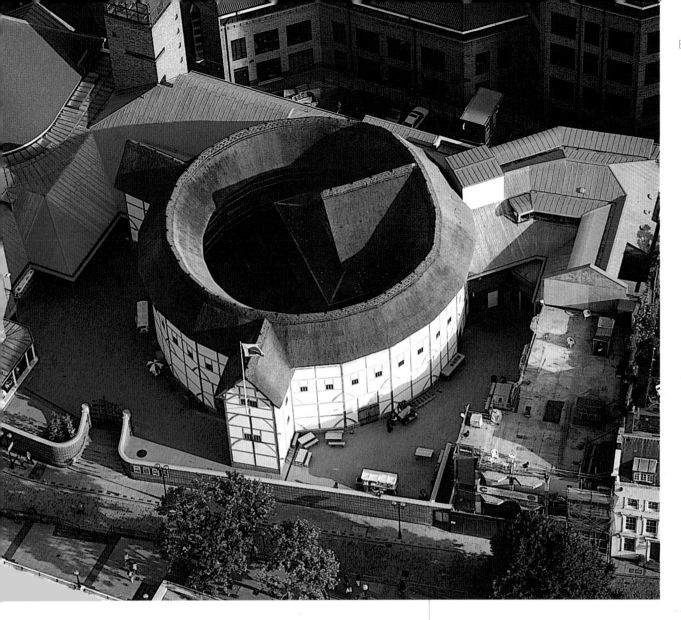

THE GLOBE THEATRE

London has maintained a reputation for high-quality theatre since the time of Shakespeare, and the Globe Theatre, faithfully recreated by American film director Sam Wanamaker close to the site of Shakespeare's original, is a fitting tribute to this reputation. The theatre also boasts the first thatched roof in London since the Great Fire of 1666.

THE ROYAL ALBERT HALL

The Albert Hall was the brainchild of Prince Albert and was to have been called the Central Hall of Arts and Sciences, but when the foundation stone was laid by Queen Victoria in 1867, she prefaced the title with the words 'Royal Albert', in homage to her husband.

THE ROYAL FESTIVAL HALL

An integral part of the South Bank Centre, the Royal Festival Hall is the only building remaining from the 1951 Festival of Britain. The curved roof above the main building is part of the auditorium, which is suspended above the open-plan foyer.

COVENT GARDEN

The two-tier market hall at the heart of the piazza in Covent Garden provides an area for shops, stallholders, buskers and street entertainers. In May 1662 Samuel Pepys watched the first recorded performance of Punch and Judy in England, which was staged in the piazza by the Italian puppeteer Pietro Gimonde.

CAFES AND PUBS

Outdoor tables give the piazza a continental feel, while elsewhere drinkers take advantage of the sunshine outside that most English of establishments, the pub. This one is named after the 15th Duke of Norfolk, whose predecessors include the 4th Duke, who planned to marry Mary Queen of Scots but was locked up in the Tower before he could do so.

SPORT

LORD'S CRICKET GROUND

Lord's, built by Yorkshireman Thomas Lord, is home to the world-famous Ashes – the story goes that when England were beaten for the first time by Australia, a mock obituary was printed in the *Sporting Times* saying that the ashes of English cricket would be taken to Australia. That winter a team went to Australia to 'recapture the ashes' and, having won the series, were presented with an urn which is believed to contain the ashes of a bail. Since then, the Ashes have been the symbolic prize for winning a Test series.

THE OVAL

The Kennington Oval is the home of Surrey County Cricket Club and was the venue for the first ever test match between England and Australia, which England won by five wickets. Traditionally the Oval stages the last match of any full Test series in England. Interestingly, soccer has also been played at the Oval; the ground staged most of the FA Cup finals between 1870 and 1892.

FAMILY SPORTS

Soccer has been dubbed 'the people's game' and it is something of a British obsession from the street to the international arena. Here, south London's Clapham Common plays host to an informal game of football and, for the unconverted, volleyball. Soccer is a corruption of the word 'association', which was used to differentiate Assocation Football from Rugby Football when the two games disagreed over rules and became two separate sports.

MARKETS

Street markets are an essential part of London's rich character, and many of them are at the heart of what used to be small communities before they were caught up in the expansion of the city. Three of the most famous are the traditional Brick Lane market (above left), trendy Camden (left) and the picturesque Columbia Road flower market (above).

SHOPPING

DESIGNER SHOPS

Floral Street in Covent Garden is home to many designer clothes shops including Paul Smith, financially Britain's most successful designer.

CAMDEN CRAFTS

Camden market caters for all tastes, from the fruit and veg stalls of Inverness Street, through the jewellery and street fashion for which Camden is most famous, to the arts and crafts stalls housed in the Victorian Market Hall (above).

LONDON
AT NIGHT

THE SOUTH BANK AT NIGHT

The River Thames reflects the lights of the city at night, with St Paul's, the NatWest Tower and the Lloyds building standing out to the north of the river, the National Theatre and the OXO Tower on the South Bank, and the distant Canada Tower in Canary Wharf in the centre of the picture.

THE SOUTH BANK

THE HAYWARD GALLERY

The quirky neon sculpture on the roof of the Hayward Gallery is by Philip Vaughan and Roger Dainton, who were commissioned by the Arts Council to build this version after a model had been shown as part the Hayward's Kinetics exhibition in 1970. The pattern of neon colours is controlled by changes in the strength and direction of the wind.

THe OXO TOWeR

The art deco tower stands on the site of an old power station which was converted into a meat packing factory by the makers of OXO cubes. In order to get round a ban on illuminated adverts, architect Albert Moore incorporated the letters into the windows of the tower so they would be lit from within.

THe LONDON IMAX

The colourful IMAX surround-cinema looks like a glass colosseum. It is the most recent addition to the South Bank's arts facilities, which include concert halls, galleries, theatres and the Museum of the Moving Image.

THE WEST END
AT NIGHT

THE WEST END

A glittering view of the West End at night (left), looking east towards the City and Docklands. In the foreground we see the British Museum and the buildings of the University of London. The Natwest Tower, the Lloyds Building and Canary Wharf are particularly impressive features of London at night. The bright lights of Piccadilly Circus and Leicester Square are guaranteed to draw crowds and entertainers to the heart of London's night life.

SOHO AND CHINATOWN

THEATRELAND

The art deco facade of the Prince Edward Theatre lights up Old Compton Street in Soho. London's Theatreland is the envy of the world – the 1,666-seat Prince Edward is a relatively recent addition whose successes include *Evita* and *Chess*.

INTERNATIONAL EATING

Take your pick from the red and gold of Gerrard Street, Chinatown's main drag, or round-the-clock espresso on Frith Street at Soho's Bar Italia.

GREENWICH
MEAN TIME

GREENWICH PARK

Greenwich has many historic buildings, including Queen's House (now home to the National Maritime Museum). The modern docklands skyline reminds us that time has moved on, with Canary Wharf and the Millennium Dome being the most notable additions to a view which Queen Mary protected by insisting that Christopher Wren build the Royal Naval Hospital in two separate halves.

THE ROYAL OBSERVATORY

A curious blend of Eastern and traditional English architecture, the onion dome of the Observatory's 28-inch refracting telescope sits on top of the Great Equatorial Building. The telescope is the largest in Britain and weighs over one and a half tons.

GREENWICH MEAN TIME

The Royal Observatory was set up in order to solve by astronomy the problem of calculating longitude, although in the end the answer lay in the accurate measurement of time. However, Greenwich retained its importance in the matter when it was internationally agreed that the Greenwich Meridian should be the Prime Meridian of the World, 0⁰ longitude. This means that the rest of the world sets its clocks in relation to Greenwich Mean Time. The new millennium began when this clock said so!

THE TIME BALL

The Old Royal Observatory is the oldest scientific institution in Britain and the oldest part of it is Flamsteed House, on the north-eastern turret of which is the bright red Time Ball. The ball rises up the mast at 12.58 each day and drops at precisely 13.00 GMT – it was added in 1833 to allow ships in the Port of London to set their chronometers accurately.

THE NATIONAL MARITIME MUSEUM

Greenwich is a particularly apt place for the National Maritime Museum – not only is it the centre of the world for navigation but it was 'the Cradle of the Navy' from the time of Henry VIII to the late 19th century and has strong connections with Britain's maritime heroes. Nelson was laid in state at Greenwich after his death at Trafalgar, and Francises Drake and Chichester were knighted here by Elizabeths I and II.

THE CUTTY SARK

A cutty sark is a short shift, as worn by the witch Nannie in Robert Burns's poem *Tam O'Shanter* – the ship's figurehead depicts Nannie clutching the tail of Tam's horse. The Cutty Sark was built in Scotland and is the world's last surviving tea clipper, although it was as a wool clipper that she really made her name, making some remarkably fast passages from Australia.

GREENWICH

Here we look down on Greenwich and the Docklands area, in one of the most exciting corners of the capital. The green of Greenwich contrasts with the industrial concentration of Docklands, where the Dome catches the light and Canary Wharf, as always, dominates the skyline.

BRITISH AIRWAYS
London eye

British Airways London Eye is conceived and designed by Marks Barfield Architects

British Airways London Eye is an attraction managed and operated by The Tussaud's Group

Opening Times
10am - 6pm

Opening times are subject to seasonal variations.

Please call 020 7654 0828 for latest opening times.

Full access and facilities for disabled visitors.

Pre-Bookings

British Airways London Eye operates a timed ticket system. Pre-book your tickets to avoid unnecessary queuing.

Tel 0870 5000 600

Payment by credit card: Visa, Mastercard, American Express, Diners Club Card.

Internet

Visit our website at:

www.ba-londoneye.com

How to Get There

We are located in Jubilee Gardens on the South Bank, between Westminster Bridge and Hungerford Bridge, opposite the Houses of Parliament.

By Tube: Waterloo - 2 minutes, Westminster - 5 minutes, Embankment - 5 minutes.

By Rail: Waterloo International Station - 5 minutes.

By Bus: Numbers 211, 24, 11.

By River: Various river boat operators utilising the new Waterloo Millennium Pier.

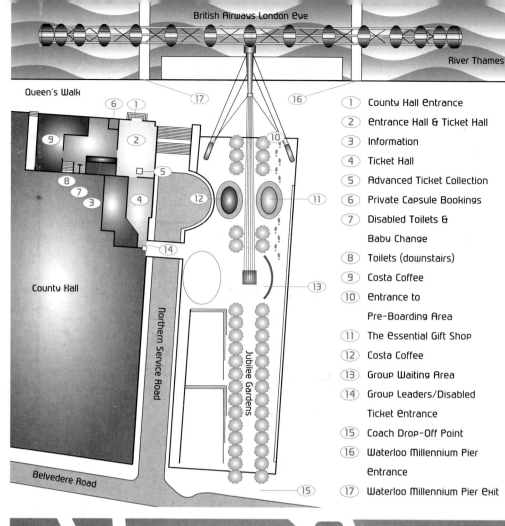

1. County Hall Entrance
2. Entrance Hall & Ticket Hall
3. Information
4. Ticket Hall
5. Advanced Ticket Collection
6. Private Capsule Bookings
7. Disabled Toilets & Baby Change
8. Toilets (downstairs)
9. Costa Coffee
10. Entrance to Pre-Boarding Area
11. The Essential Gift Shop
12. Costa Coffee
13. Group Waiting Area
14. Group Leaders/Disabled Ticket Entrance
15. Coach Drop-Off Point
16. Waterloo Millennium Pier Entrance
17. Waterloo Millennium Pier Exit

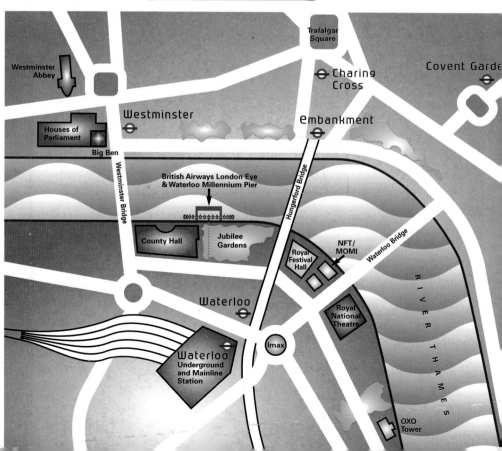